THE FRUGAL GOURMET
DESK DIARY 1990

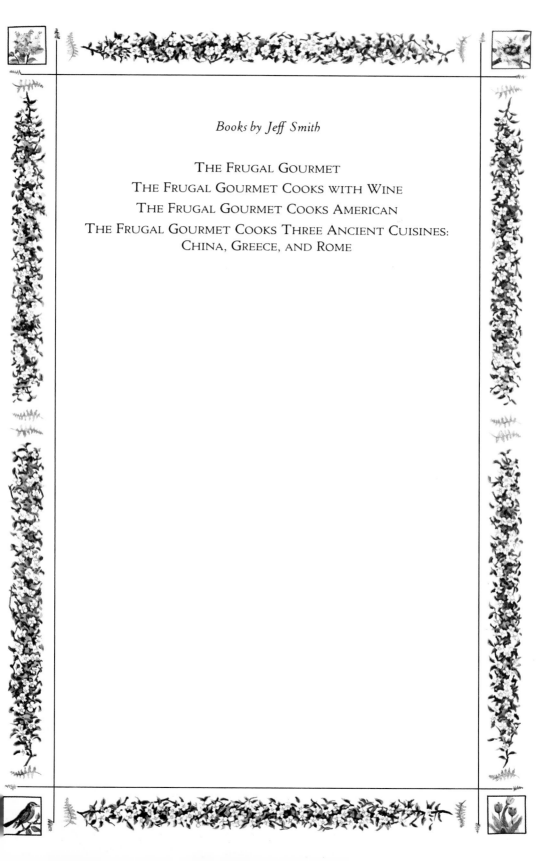

Books by Jeff Smith

THE FRUGAL GOURMET

THE FRUGAL GOURMET COOKS WITH WINE

THE FRUGAL GOURMET COOKS AMERICAN

THE FRUGAL GOURMET COOKS THREE ANCIENT CUISINES:
CHINA, GREECE, AND ROME

THE
FRUGAL
GOURMET
DESK DIARY 1990

JEFF SMITH

Illustrations by Chris Cart

QUILL
WILLIAM MORROW
New York

Book design by Richard Oriolo

ISBN 0-688-08612-8

Printed in the United States of America

First Edition

1 2 3 4 5 6 7 8 9 10

CAVIAR MOLD

SERVES 12 TO 16
AT A COCKTAIL PARTY

This is a very easy dish that will add serious elegance to your party buffet.

6 *eggs, hard-boiled and peeled*

1 *envelope gelatin*

2 *tablespoons cool water*

2 *tablespoons lemon juice*

1/8 *teaspoon salt*

1/8 *teaspoon Tabasco*

1/2 *small yellow onion, peeled and chopped fine*

1 *teaspoon Worcestershire sauce*

3/4 *cup mayonnaise*

1 *jar (3 ounces) Danish black lumpfish caviar*

Chopped parsley for garnish

Grind or grate the eggs fine, and allow them to cool.

Dissolve the gelatin in the water. Place in a very small saucepan, and add the lemon juice. Stir over low heat until the gelatin dissolves completely.

Place the eggs, salt, Tabasco, onion, Worcestershire sauce, and mayonnaise in a bowl. Blend well, and then add the lemon and gelatin mixture. Mix again. Finally, very gently stir in the caviar. Do not stir much because you will discolor the mixture.

Pour into a 1-quart mold, and refrigerate. Unmold, and garnish with parsley.

Serve with crackers.

Sunday

Monday **1**

Tuesday **2**

Wednesday **3**

Thursday **4**

FIRST QUARTER

Friday **5**

Saturday **6**

EPIPHANY

STEAMING DEVICES

There are many devices for steaming and many foods that respond beautifully to this sensible and efficient method of quick cooking.

STAINLESS STEEL BASKET STEAMER: This is best for vegetables and is available in any department or hardware store.

CHINESE BAMBOO STEAMER: This uses several layers and will not allow water to drip on your food. This is my favorite steaming gadget.

ALUMINUM CHINESE STEAMER: This is like the above, but moisture will condense on your food.

RED CLAY STEAMER FROM HUNAN, CHINA: This looks like an angel food pan with a lid; sits atop a pot of boiling water. Expensive, but it is attractive, and it works very well. Serve from the cooker.

MY CHEAP STEAMER: Remove the bottom and the top from a small tuna fish can, and place middle section in the bottom of a deep kettle. Add a couple of inches of water to the bottom of the kettle, and place the heatproof bowl of food to be cooked on the top of the tuna can. Place a towel over the top of the kettle to catch dripping or condensing water; place the lid on the pot, and bring the ends of the towel up onto the top of the pot. Hold in place with an upside-down cup.

Sunday *7*

Monday *8*

Tuesday *9*

Wednesday *10*

FULL MOON

Thursday *11*

Friday *12*

Saturday *13*

FISH STEAMED WITH LEMON

SERVES 4 TO 6

People who dislike the fishy flavor of fish will enjoy this dish because the cooked lemon cleanses the flavor. Very easy and very delicious.

This method of cooking fish works for just about any kind of fillet that you wish to use.

1 *pound fresh fish fillets*	*Freshly ground black pepper*
2 *tablespoons or less light soy sauce*	*Thin lemon slices*

Place the fish in a steaming bowl, and add the soy along with a bit of black pepper. Top with several slices, very thin slices, of lemon. Steam for about 20 minutes.

STEAMED VEGETABLES, MIXED

You can try any vegetables you wish. The point here is to stop boiling vegetables in gallons of water and simply to steam them, without any water. Very rich flavor.

Very thin carrot sticks	*Melted butter*
Very thin zucchini sticks	

Blend vegetables with a bit of melted butter, and steam until tender. Should take no more than 14 minutes.

Sunday **14**

Monday **15**

MARTIN LUTHER KING, JR.,'S BIRTHDAY *(Observed)*

Tuesday **16**

Wednesday **17**

Thursday **18**

LAST QUARTER

Friday **19**

Saturday **20**

PORK DUMPLINGS WITH HOT SAUCE

In the northern regions of China, noodles of every form are relished in the winter, along with enough pepper sauce to keep you warm.

SAUCE

2 *tablespoons soy sauce (Kikkoman)*

1 *tablespoon Japanese rice wine vinegar*

1 *teaspoon red chili and garlic paste*

1 *teaspoon sesame oil*

1 *tablespoon chopped green onion*

³/₄ *pound ground lean pork*

¹/₂ *tablespoon cornstarch*

1 *tablespoon Chinese rice wine or dry sherry*

2 *tablespoons light soy sauce*

1 *teaspoon grated fresh ginger*

2 *cloves garlic, crushed*

4 *green onions or scallions, chopped*

1 *tablespoon sesame oil*

1 *egg, beaten*

1 *teaspoon freshly ground black pepper*

¹/₂ *teaspoon salt*

4 *cups cabbage, chopped fine and drained well*

1 *package wonton wrappers*

Mix the sauce ingredients together and set aside. Mix all the other ingredients, with the exception of the cabbage and the wrappers. Mix in a bowl by hand, stirring the mixture until it holds together well. Using a towel, squeeze all the moisture you can out of the cabbage. (I use a potato ricer.) Stir the cabbage into the meat mixture.

Place ¹/₂ tablespoon of the filling in the center of a wonton noodle. With your finger, wet two adjoining sides of the noodle with a bit of tap water. Keep a cup of water handy for this. Fold the opposite sides over on top of the two moistened edges, thus giving you a triangle. Seal carefully. Be sure to press out all the air bubbles or the noodle will explode.

To cook, drop the noodles into boiling water and stir very gently with a wooden spoon so that they do not stick together. After a few minutes, they will float to the top. Cook them 1 more minute and then remove them with a slotted spoon.

Serve several in a bowl for each guest. Allow the guest to put on his own sauce.

Sunday 21

Monday 22

Tuesday 23

Wednesday 24

Thursday 25

Friday 26

NEW MOON

Saturday 27

CHINESE NEW YEAR *(The Year of the Horse)*

OLD-FASHIONED RICE PUDDING

SERVES 6 TO 8

We know that this dish was popular with the likes of Thomas Jefferson and other forefathers and foremothers. People don't seem to be making it much anymore and that saddens me. It is little work and just delicious, cold, in the middle of the night.

1½ cups milk
Pinch of salt
5 tablespoons sugar
1 tablespoon butter, melted
1 teaspoon vanilla
5 eggs, beaten

¼ cup brandy
2 cups cooked long-grain rice
1 tablespoon fresh lemon juice
Cinnamon for topping

Mix all ingredients except the rice and lemon juice and cinnamon. Mix them well and then add the rice and lemon juice. Sprinkle a bit of cinnamon on top. Place in a 8 × 10-inch greased baking dish and bake at 325° for 50 minutes, or until lightly brown and the custard is set. Test with a table knife. Stick it in the center of the dish, and if it comes out clean, the dish is baked.

In earlier times maple syrup was served on top of this pudding. Milk is enjoyed as well.

HINT: ON COOKING RICE When cooking rice, use a heavy saucepan. If your pans are light stainless steel, use a heat diffuser. It will help keep the heat even under thin pans.

Sunday **28**

Monday **29**

Tuesday **30**

Wednesday **31**

Thursday **1**

Friday **2**

GROUND HOG DAY
FIRST QUARTER

Karen J's Birthday

Saturday **3**

CHICKEN WITH MUSHROOM SOUP

SERVES 6 TO 8

What to do with that little bit of leftover chicken? This is a snap, and after all, soups should lengthen the time that you spend at table with your friends or family. Such a good use for a cup of chicken.

½ cup sliced fresh mushrooms
2 tablespoons butter
6 cups Chicken Soup Stock

1 cup cooked chicken
½ cup white rice, uncooked
2 tablespoons lemon juice
Chopped green onions for garnish

Sauté the mushrooms in the butter. Add to the soup stock along with the chicken and rice. Cook until the rice is puffy, and serve with a little lemon juice and chopped green onions in a bowl.

CHICKEN SOUP STOCK

MAKES ABOUT 2½ QUARTS

If you have a bit of this in your refrigerator, you will think of marvelous soups to make. Jews call this *Gildern yoich*, or golden soup.

3 pounds chicken necks and backs
4 celery stalks, chopped into large pieces
6 carrots, chopped into large pieces

2 yellow onions, peeled and chopped into large pieces
Salt and freshly ground black pepper to taste

Boil the chicken necks and backs in water to cover. Add the celery, carrots, and yellow onions. Add salt and pepper. Simmer for 2 hours. Strain and refrigerate.

HINT: TO REMOVE FAT FROM THE TOP OF SOUP STOCK
Use a plastic tube. Plastic tubing about ⅓ inch in diameter can be purchased at hardware stores. Strain the stock, and then remove the stock from beneath the fat by siphoning with the plastic tube. Tip the kettle holding the stock so that you can always keep the siphoning tube beneath the level of the fat. This works very well.

FEBRUARY

Sunday **4**

Monday **5**

Tuesday **6**

Wednesday **7**

Thursday **8**

Friday **9**

FULL MOON

Saturday **10**

BEEF STEW, PEASANT STYLE

SERVES 6 TO 8

This dish is common in terms of history . . . but delicious in terms of the table. Allow everything to marinate overnight so that the blending of flavors results in a wonderful and smooth flavor. Remember, marinating in wine really does tenderize meat. And please note that this dish does not need salt. The use of wine will help you cut down on your need for the taste of salt in food.

- 2 pounds beef chuck roast
- 2 carrots, unpeeled, sliced
- 3 celery stalks, sliced
- 1 large yellow onion, peeled and sliced
- 3 garlic cloves, crushed
- 1 teaspoon freshly ground pepper
- ½ teaspoon whole thyme leaves
- 1 bay leaf
- ½ teaspoon whole rosemary leaves
- 3 cups Zinfandel
- 3 tablespoons olive oil
- 2 tablespoons tomato paste

Place all ingredients, except olive oil and tomato paste, in a glass or ceramic casserole. Or you can use an iron casserole if it is covered with porcelain enamel. Cover and place in the refrigerator for 24 hours.

The next day, remove the meat from the marinade, saving everything. Heat a heavy frying pan and add the oil. Brown the meat over high heat, using small batches so that the pan is not crowded. Return the meat to the casserole containing the wine and vegetables and add the tomato paste. Bring to a boil and then place in a 350° oven, covered, for 1½ to 2 hours. Meat should be tender.

Remove the meat to a warm platter. Purée the sauce and vegetables in a food processor or run them through a sieve. Return to the casserole and bring the sauce to a boil, skim off the fat, and correct the seasoning. Be careful with the salt!

I like this with semolina dumplings, along with a green salad with garlic dressing.

WINE SUGGESTION: Zinfandel.

Sunday **11**

Monday **12**

LINCOLN'S BIRTHDAY

Tuesday **13**

Wednesday **14**

VALENTINE'S DAY

Thursday **15**

Friday **16**

Saturday **17**

LAST QUARTER

MARTHA'S VIRGINIA CAKE

MAKES 2 CAKES

The General had a special fondness for this cake. The family referred to it as "Virginia whiskey cake," but the only recipes that I could find used red wine and brandy . . . not whiskey. This recipe came from the hand of Mrs. Washington's granddaughter and it did not mention whiskey at all. I expect that Ms. Custis, the step-granddaughter of General Washington, was not too keen on the fact that the old boy had a large rye whiskey still and traded whiskey in the West Indies for special food products that he loved to eat at Mount Vernon, products such as bananas and coconut. He also drank the rye whiskey. So, in a fit of questionable historical research, I have restored the whiskey to this cake. I believe that the father of our land would approve.

1 *stick soft butter*	1 *cup sweet port wine*
½ *cup sugar*	¼ *cup brandy*
3 *cups flour*	1½ *cups diced dried mixed*
2 *teaspoons baking powder*	*fruit (for fruitcake)*
⅛ *teaspoon freshly grated nutmeg*	6 *eggs, separated*
¼ *teaspoon mace*	1 *cup whiskey*

Cream the butter and sugar until smooth. Beat in the yolks, one at a time.

Mix the flour, baking powder, and spices together. Stir the flour mixture into the egg/sugar mixture. Mix in the port and the brandy. Stir in the dried fruit.

Whip the egg whites until they form very soft peaks. Stir in about a quarter of them to lighten the batter. Fold in the remaining egg whites very gently.

Bake in a preheated 325° oven in 2 loaf pans for 1 hour, or until a toothpick stuck into the middle of the cakes comes out clean.

Cool the cakes and pour half of the whiskey over each. Cover each pan with aluminum foil and allow to sit for a day before serving.

Sunday **18**

Monday **19**

PRESIDENT'S DAY *(Observed)*

Tuesday **20**

Wednesday **21**

Thursday **22**

WASHINGTON'S BIRTHDAY

Friday **23**

Saturday **24**

CUBAN BLACK BEANS
SERVES 4

I hope you don't have trouble finding these beans. They are worth the effort, I promise. If you serve them over rice with a green salad on the side, you have a complete and interesting meal. I had this dish in Miami one evening, and I have made it often since.

- ½ pound black beans or turtle beans, soaked overnight
- 4 stalks celery, chopped
- 1 large yellow onion, peeled and chopped
- 1 pound ham hocks, cut into 2-inch pieces
- 1 teaspoon crushed red pepper flakes
- 2 bay leaves
- ¼ cup parsley, chopped
- Tabasco to taste
- Salt and freshly ground black pepper to taste

Drain the water from the beans, and place all the ingredients in a cooking pot with a tight-fitting lid. Barely cover with fresh water, and simmer for 1 hour, or until tender. Remember that you should not add salt to this dish until it is ready to serve because the ham hocks add salt to the dish.

Serve over cooked long-grain white rice.

Sunday 25

NEW MOON

Monday 26

Tuesday 27

MARDI GRAS

Wednesday 28

ASH WEDNESDAY

Thursday 1

Friday 2

Saturday 3

FIRST QUARTER

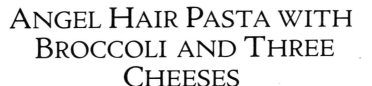

ANGEL HAIR PASTA WITH BROCCOLI AND THREE CHEESES

SERVES 3 OR 4

I have fallen in love with a restaurant just off Michigan Avenue in Chicago. It serves northern Italian food and is called Avanzare. The pasta is made fresh on the premises, and the chef is very creative. This dish came as an inspiration after I had tasted most of his menu.

2 cloves garlic, crushed

2 tablespoons olive oil

½ yellow onion, peeled and chopped

½ pound broccoli, flowerets only

⅓ cup whipping cream

Freshly ground black pepper to taste

Salt to taste (optional)

½ pound angel hair pasta

¼ pound Swiss cheese, grated

4 tablespoons Romano cheese, grated

3 tablespoons Mizithra cheese, grated

Chopped parsley for garnish (optional)

Sauté the garlic in the oil until it just begins to brown. Add the yellow onion and the broccoli flowerets (i.e., the tops of the spears), and sauté until the broccoli is barely tender.

Add the cream and pepper. You may add salt if you wish.

In the meantime, cook the angel hair pasta for just a few minutes in salted boiling water. Watch this carefully because the pasta cooks in very little time. Drain the pasta, and toss with the three cheeses. Add the cream and the vegetables, toss, and serve.

You may wish to garnish this with more cheese on top. Some parsley might be nice as well.

MARCH

Sunday 4

Monday 5

Tuesday 6

Wednesday 7

Thursday 8

Friday 9

Saturday 10

FRIED CABBAGE

SERVES 5 TO 6

Sounds as if we have really hit rock bottom, doesn't it? Cabbage is a wonderful food if you do not cook it long, and it is very good for you. I love this recipe.

4 strips bacon, diced

2 garlic cloves, crushed (optional)

1 large yellow onion, peeled and sliced

2 pounds cabbage, cored and sliced

½ teaspoon caraway seeds

½ cup Chicken Soup Stock (below) or boullion

½ cup dry white wine

Salt and freshly ground black pepper to taste

Heat a large Dutch oven and add the bacon. Sauté until cooked, but not crisp. Add the garlic and onion. Sauté until the onion is clear. Add the cabbage, caraway, stock, and wine. Cover and cook until the cabbage collapses, about 5 minutes. Remove the lid and cook until the liquid is reduced a bit, about 10 minutes, stirring now and then. The cabbage should be barely tender. Do not overcook it.

VARIATION: If you wish to avoid the bacon, use 3 tablespoons olive oil instead.

CHICKEN SOUP STOCK

MAKES ABOUT 2½ QUARTS

If you have a bit of this in your refrigerator, you will think of marvelous soups to make. Jews call this *Gildern yoich,* or golden soup.

3 pounds chicken necks and backs

4 celery stalks, chopped into large pieces

6 carrots, chopped into large pieces

2 yellow onions, peeled and chopped into large pieces

Salt and freshly ground black pepper to taste

Boil the chicken necks and backs in water to cover. Add the celery, carrots, and yellow onions. Add salt and pepper. Simmer for 2 hours. Strain and refrigerate.

Sunday **11**

FULL MOON

Monday **12**

Tuesday **13**

Wednesday **14**

Thursday **15**

Friday **16**

Saturday **17**

ST. PATRICK'S DAY

BAKED FISH
IN VINEGAR SAUCE

SERVES 5 TO 8

This is actually fish in salad dressing, and it will startle the children in your house who claim that they don't like fish.

2 or 3 *pounds whitefish fillets*
Flour
Salt
2 *large yellow onions, peeled and sliced thin*
Butter
1/2 *cup olive oil*
1/2 *cup white wine vinegar*

2 *cloves garlic, crushed*
1 *teaspoon oregano*
2 *teaspoons dry mustard*
Handful of chopped parsley
1/2 *teaspoon ground coriander*
1 *tablespoon lemon juice*
1/4 *cup dry white wine*

Dredge the fish fillets in flour and a tiny bit of salt. Place them in a shallow baking dish so that they all fit snugly. Sauté the onions in a bit of butter until they are tender and transparent. Spread the onions over the fish fillets. Prepare something akin to a good salad dressing as follows: Blend the olive oil, wine vinegar, garlic, oregano, mustard, parsley, coriander, lemon juice, and wine (you may wish to add some other favorite ingredient such as dill, in which case you could omit the coriander). Pour the dressing over the fish, and bake the fish, uncovered, in a 350° oven for about 45 minutes.

Serve a nice soup, followed by a pasta, then the fish with a salad on the side. Perfect dinnertime!

HINT: HOW DO YOU CHECK TO SEE IF FISH IS FRESH? There are several things that you can check to be sure that fish is fresh: (1) The eyes should be clean and bulging, shiny and bright; this is probably the most important test. (2) Lift the gills of the fish, and check to see that they are red and clean-looking, never brown or pale. (3) If the fish is fresh, the flesh will be elastic and firm, rather than soggy or soft. (4) The scales should be tight and bright, not falling off. (5) The fish should smell not "fishy" but fresh and clean.

Sunday **18**

Monday **19**

LAST QUARTER

Tuesday **20**

VERNAL EQUINOX

Wednesday **21**

Thursday **22**

Friday **23**

Saturday **24**

BASIC OMELET

3 eggs, at room temperature
1 tablespoon water
½ tablespoon peanut oil
½ tablespoon butter

Salt and freshly ground
black pepper to taste
Chopped parsley for garnish

Heat the pan on medium high.

Whip the eggs in a small bowl with a table fork. Add the water, and whip again.

Place the oil and butter in the pan at the same time. When the butter stops foaming, whip the eggs a couple of times, and pour them into the pan. When the omelet begins to set, you may have to lift the edge with a wooden spatula and allow the wet portion of the mixture to run under the omelet. Add salt and pepper if you wish.*

Slide the omelet onto a plate and, holding the handle backhand, fold the omelet over in half, using the pan. Garnish with parsley or some of the filling and serve hot.

SUGGESTED FILLINGS: Sautéed mushrooms; ham and swiss cheese; sautéed vegetables (such as green onions, green peppers, tomatoes, along with a bit of basil or oregano); strawberry jam and sour cream for a dessert omelet; stews or leftover spaghetti

*Before salt and pepper are added, any filling may be added. Place it on the front half of the omelet (the handle of the pan is considered the back portion).

HINT: THE BASIC RULES FOR A GOOD OMELET
1. Use butter and peanut oil in your cooking. The blend of the two will prevent the butter from burning and will give the eggs fine flavor and color.
2. Have the eggs at room temperature. Always have a dozen eggs sitting in a bowl on the counter. They will keep fine for two weeks in the refrigerator and for several days on the counter.
3. Never put salt in the egg mixture. It toughens the eggs. Add the salt just before folding.
4. Never use milk in the egg mixture. Use only water. Milk makes your omelet watery since it will not blend with the eggs. Water blends and helps keep the omelet high.
5. Heat the pan before you put in the peanut oil and butter. When the butter stops foaming, add the eggs.

Sunday **25**

Monday **26**

NEW MOON

Tuesday **27**

Wednesday **28**

Thursday **29**

Friday **30**

Saturday **31**

LEBANESE BREAD

MAKES
12 TO 15 LOAVES

When I was a child, my Lebanese uncle's mother died. Since he was the oldest son in the family, my uncle was given the responsibility of making the family bread for the rest of the brothers, sisters, and even cousins. The passing of the bread paddles was a most important event. This is as close to his recipe as I can come, and once you have learned to make this, you will never buy pocket bread or pita from a bakery again.

> 2 *cakes yeast*
> 2 *cups lukewarm water*
> 8 *cups unbleached white flour*
>
> 2 *cups whole wheat flour*
> ½ *tablespoon salt*

Dissolve the yeast in the water. Place the flours in a large bowl. Mix in the salt. Pour in the yeast and water mixture, and add enough water to make a very stiff dough. Knead until smooth. Cover, and let rise until doubled. Punch down, and mold dough into small pieces about 3 inches in diameter. Be sure to seal the dough by rolling it around in your hands until it is smooth. Place on a tray; cover with plastic wrap; allow to rise for 1 hour.

Preheat your oven. It must be at 525° minimum. Fun to have a glass door so you can see. Roll out balls of dough on a floured board, one at a time, into pancakelike circles 8 to 9 inches in diameter. Place on a small wooden board and slide onto upside-down cookie sheet in oven. While one loaf is baking, roll out the next. The loaf takes only a few minutes to bake. Very light brown spots will form on the loaf after it has puffed up like a ball. Remove it from the oven, and place on a terry-cloth towel. Cover the bread with another towel, and stack the loaves one on top of the other as they come from the oven. Keep covered until cool.

Sunday **1**

APRIL FOOL'S DAY
DAYLIGHT SAVING TIME BEGINS

Monday **2**

FIRST QUARTER

Tuesday **3**

Wednesday **4**

Thursday **5**

Friday **6**

Saturday **7**

MATZO BALL SOUP

SERVES 6

This dish is heaven! When I was in graduate school, I became absolutely addicted to the matzo ball soup served at the Stage Delicatessen in Manhattan. This one is just as good, and it is not hard to make. I found it years ago on the Manischewitz matzo meal box.

SOUP STOCK

3 pounds chicken backs and necks, rinsed, with fat pulled off the backs and reserved

3 carrots, chopped

1 large yellow onion, peeled and chopped

4 stalks celery, chopped

2 quarts water

6 peppercorns

1 teaspoon salt or more to taste

MATZO BALLS

Reserved chicken fat

2 eggs, slightly beaten

1/2 cup matzo meal

1 teaspoon salt

2 tablespoons soup stock

Chopped parsley for garnish

Cover, and simmer the soup stock ingredients for 2 hours. Drain the stock, and remove the fat; or chill and remove the next day.

Place the chicken fat in a small frying pan. Heat gently over medium heat until the fat is rendered from the solid part and the remains are small and lightly browned. Do not burn the fat. (Some people attempt to make matzo balls with oil or margarine, but the flavor is simply not the same.)

Cool the fat, and mix 2 tablespoons of the clear fat with the eggs. Mix together the matzo meal and salt, and add to the eggs. When all is well blended, add the 2 tablespoons of soup stock. Cover the mixing bowl, and refrigerate for at least 20 minutes. Using a 2- or 3-quart pot, bring salted water to a brisk boil. Roll the cold mixture into 12 balls, and place on wax paper. When all the balls are complete, drop them into the slightly boiling water, cover, and cook for 30 to 40 minutes. Have the soup at room temperature, and place the drained matzo balls in the soup pot. When you are ready to serve, heat the soup at a simmer for about 5 minutes.

To serve, place two balls in each bowl of soup. Garnish with a bit of chopped parsley.

APRIL

Sunday **8**

PALM SUNDAY

Monday **9**

NEW MOON

Tuesday **10**

FIRST DAY OF PASSOVER

Wednesday **11**

Thursday **12**

Friday **13**

GOOD FRIDAY

Saturday **14**

Leg of Lamb
in Balsamic Vinegar
SERVES 4 TO 6

Balsamic vinegar is a wonderfully aged product from Modena, in Italy. It is unlike most wine vinegars in that the flavor is so mild. Normally, I would not urge you to use vinegars when you are going to serve a good wine, since the vinegars fight and get in the way of the flavor of the wine. In this case, however, the flavor of the vinegar is mild to begin with, and the roasting calms it down to a very mellow flavor. You will enjoy this easily prepared dish. The only thing that might get in your way is the fact that it must be marinated for five hours.

1 5- to 6-pound leg of lamb
1/4 cup olive oil
1/4 cup balsamic vinegar
  Salt and freshly ground
  black pepper to taste
1/2 tablespoon dried whole
  rosemary leaves, or twice
  that much if fresh
2 garlic cloves, crushed

Using a sharp-pointed knife or a pot fork, pierce the leg in several places and soak it for 5 hours in the olive oil mixed with the vinegar.

Remove the lamb from the marinade and reserve the marinade. Place the lamb on a roasting rack and rub with the salt, pepper, rosemary, and garlic. Place a meat thermometer in the thickest part of the leg. Be sure you do not touch the bone. Bake at 325° until the thermometer reaches 140°. This should take about 1 1/4 to 1 3/4 hours. Baste with the marinade several times during the roasting. Remove from the oven and let sit 1/2 hour before carving. The lamb will continue to cook a bit. Slice at the table or buffet.

Risotto with vegetables and a green salad with garlic dressing would complete a fine meal.

WINE SUGGESTION: Italian Barolo or California Cabernet.

Sunday **15**

Monday **16**

EASTER MONDAY *(Canada)*

Tuesday **17**

Wednesday **18**

LAST QUARTER

Thursday **19**

Friday **20**

Saturday **21**

PASTITSO

SERVES 6 TO 8

This is Greek lasagne, but I hesitate to use the Italian term. The Greeks were making this dish before the Italians began with their noodle dishes. And the sauce used in this dish, a basic white sauce, is also Greek, though it is known by its French name, béchamel.

- 2 pounds hamburger
- 1 large yellow onion, peeled and chopped
- 2 tablespoons olive oil
- ½ cup chopped parsley
- 1 clove garlic, crushed
- ½ teaspoon ground cinnamon
- 1 can (8 ounces) tomato sauce

- ½ cup white wine
- 1 pound lasagne noodles
- ¼ pound butter, melted
- 3 eggs, beaten
  Freshly grated Parmesan cheese
- 4 cups Béchamel Sauce for Pastitso (below)

Sauté the hamburger along with the yellow onion in the oil. When the onions are clear, add the parsley, garlic, cinnamon, tomato sauce, and white wine. Let this cook together gently for 30 minutes.

Meanwhile, boil the lasagne noodles until not quite tender. Drain, and soak in cold water to keep them from sticking together.

When the sauce is done, drain the cold noodles, and place in a large bowl. Add the butter, 3 eggs, and a handful of Parmesan cheese. Toss the noodles, and place half the mixture in a buttered baking dish. Add the meat sauce. Place the rest of the noodles on top, and cover with the béchamel sauce. Top with more grated cheese. Bake at 350° for about 1 hour, or until the top is bubbly.

BÉCHAMEL SAUCE

MAKES 4 CUPS

- 4 cups milk
- ½ cup butter
- 6 tablespoons flour

Salt and freshly ground black pepper to taste

Pinch or two ground cinnamon

Heat the milk. Melt the butter, and stir in the flour. Stir the flour and butter into the hot milk, and continue stirring, until thick. Add the salt, pepper, and cinnamon.

Sunday 22

Monday 23

Tuesday 24

NEW MOON

Wednesday 25

Thursday 26

Friday 27

ARBOR DAY

Saturday 28

RULES FOR COOKING MUSHROOMS

Do not wash unless you have to.
Do not peel.
Do not soak.
Do not overcook.

TYPES OF MUSHROOMS AVAILABLE

WHITE MEADOW MUSHROOM: fresh in all supermarkets.

DRIED EUROPEAN MUSHROOM: cepé, boletus, or porcini. These are delicious, but if they come from Europe, they will be terribly expensive. Find an Italian market that brings them in from South America, and you will pay only somewhere between $10 and $14 a pound. The real Italian dried mushroom will cost you a fortune! You may also find some that are domestic. In any case, keep them in a tightly sealed jar at the back of your refrigerator, where they will keep for a year.

CHANTERELLE: the most elegant of the wild mushrooms. Can be purchased dried or canned, rarely fresh because no one is willing to give them up!

MOREL: dark-capped beauty. Canned or dried.

JAPANESE ENOKI-DAKE: fresh, tiny, slender-stalked. Expensive but very "in" with the nouvelle cuisine crowd as a garnish.

CHINESE BLACK: dried. Soak in tepid water for 1 hour before use. Not expensive if you buy them in a Chinese market.

JAPANESE SHIITAKI: very similar to Chinese black. Dried; some supermarkets carry them fresh. Expensive.

CHINESE STRAW MUSHROOM: so tender sometimes called a jelly mushroom. Very fragile. You will see them only canned.

CLOUD'S EARS: Chinese black fungus. Look like wood chips when purchased, but when soaked, they become delicious and tender. They can also be purchased in white and are called silver ears. A less expensive and thicker version of the tree fungus is also black and called Juda's ears. All must be soaked before being cooked.

Sunday **29**

Monday **30**

Tuesday **1**

FIRST QUARTER

Wednesday **2**

Thursday **3**

Friday **4**

Saturday **5**

JAMBALAYA
SERVES 8

Originally this dish, like so many dishes that have become classics, was designed to use up leftovers. The dish stands in that great tradition of frugal cooks who could not afford to throw anything away, or, in the more profound tradition, that good community of cooks who *refused* to throw out any edible leftovers. This bit of Cajun ingenuity is now common all over New Orleans, and there are as many variations on this dish as any one I know.

2 pounds pork spareribs, cut into single-bone pieces

3 tablespoons peanut oil

1 large yellow onion, peeled and chopped

2 green peppers, cored and chopped

3 cloves garlic, peeled and chopped fine

4 celery stalks, chopped

6 green onions, chopped

1 can (28 ounces) whole tomatoes, crushed by hand

3½ cups canned chicken broth

½ pound smoked hot-link sausage, sliced in ¼-inch pieces

1 cup diced ham

3 tablespoons chopped parsley

2 teaspoons Tabasco

¼ cup Worcestershire sauce

3 teaspoons whole thyme leaves

Salt and freshly ground black pepper to taste

2 cups uncooked converted rice

Place the spareribs on a broiling rack and bake them in a 400° oven until brown, about 15 to 20 minutes. Set aside.

In the meantime heat a large frying pan and add the oil. Sauté the yellow onion, green peppers, garlic, celery, and green onion until all are tender. Place the vegetables and the ribs in a 12-quart stockpot, along with the tomatoes and chicken stock. Cover and simmer for 1 hour.

Pan-fry the sliced sausage until it just begins to brown. Deglaze the pan with a bit of the broth and add the pan drippings to the stockpot. Set the sausage aside.

Add the remaining ingredients, except the sausage and rice, and simmer, covered, for another 20 minutes. Add the sausage and rice and simmer for 25 minutes. Correct the seasoning and serve.

MAY

Sunday **6**

mom D's B-day

Monday **7**

MAY DAY

Tuesday **8**

Wednesday **9**

Jeff's B-day
FULL MOON

Thursday **10**

Friday **11**

Saturday **12**

MOM'S BASIC WAFFLE BATTER

MAKES 4 TO 5 WAFFLES

We would often have waffles for dinner when I was a child. I suppose you have the same story. They were crispy and delicious. Once in a while we would have fresh strawberries on top, or perhaps freshly picked wild mountain blackberries. I have the recipe that Mom used to use but mine were never quite so crisp and wonderful. I finally figured out what was wrong. Mom always used an old-fashioned electric waffle iron, the kind to which the first waffle *always* stuck. It never failed. Now we have a Teflon-coated waffle iron and nothing sticks . . . and the waffles are always soggy. If you can, find an old waffle iron at a garage sale and clean it up. Spray it with Pam and you will have no problem . . . and the waffles will crunch. My mother bought a new waffle iron a few years ago and she has been most unhappy with it. I found her an old one the other day at a junk shop in Chicago. I hauled it home on the plane and presented it to her. She feels better and the waffles are crunchy again.

1³/₄ cups all-purpose flour
2 teaspoons baking powder
¹/₂ teaspoon salt
1 tablespoon sugar
3 egg yolks, beaten

4 tablespoons melted butter or oil
1¹/₂ cups milk
3 egg whites, beaten until stiff

Mix the dry ingredients together. I use my electric mixer for this. Mix the egg yolks, melted butter or oil, and milk together and blend into the dry mixture. Do not overmix. Fold in, most gently, the beaten egg whites.

NOTE: My frugal mother would often use sour milk in this recipe. In that case she would add a bit of baking soda, perhaps 1 teaspoon.

MAY

Sunday **13**

Monday **14**

Tuesday **15**

Wednesday **16**

Thursday **17**

LAST QUARTER

Friday **18**

Saturday **19**

ARMED FORCES DAY

ASPARAGUS QUICHE
SERVES 4 TO 6

I like this best with fresh asparagus. During asparagus season our family enjoys this lovely vegetable daily, and this is a favorite dinner.

- 1 *pound fresh asparagus or 1 package frozen asparagus spears*
- 2 *tablespoons butter*
- 1 *Quiche Crust baked and cooled*
- 4 *eggs, beaten*
- ¾ *cup cream*
- 1¼ *cups milk*
- ¼ *teaspoon dried dill weed*
- *Salt and freshly ground black pepper to taste*

Clean the asparagus, or defrost and drain the frozen asparagus. Cut up into inch-long pieces, and sauté in the butter to remove some of the moisture. The asparagus should be tender and green, not soft.

Place the asparagus in the bottom of the crust. Mix the eggs, cream, milk, dill weed, salt, and pepper. Fill the crust, and bake at 375° for 30 to 40 minutes, or until a knife inserted into the center of the pie comes out dry. Cool for 10 minutes before cutting. Can also be served at room temperature. Serve it with a salad and very dry white wine.

QUICHE CRUST
MAKES 2 9-INCH CRUSTS OR 1 LARGER CRUST

- 2 *cups flour*
- 2 *teaspoons baking powder*
- *Salt (optional)*
- ½ *cup vegetable oil*
- ¼ *cup milk*

Mix the flour and the baking powder together. Add salt if you wish. Mix the oil and milk together, and then pour into the flour. Stir only until mixed. The mixture will be rather coarse and granular, but it will roll out well. Do not overmix. Mold into two balls, and wrap with plastic. Allow to sit for 15 minutes. Each ball will make one 9-inch piecrust. If you are using a larger French quiche pan, then use a bit more dough. Roll out between two sheets of wax paper.

Place the pastry in the quiche pan or pie plate, and prick the bottom with a kitchen fork. Line the inside with wax paper or aluminum foil. Put two cups of dry beans into the piecrust, and bake at 400° for 12 minutes.

Sunday **20**

Monday **21**

Tuesday **22**

Wednesday **23**

Thursday **24**

NEW MOON

Friday **25**

Greg & Pam's Wedding

Saturday **26**

MUFFALETTA FROM NEW ORLEANS

SERVES 6

There is still a battle going on in New Orleans over who invented this dish. It does not matter. All that matters is that you make the olive salad the day ahead . . . with plenty of garlic.

This is a great buffet dish because you can put out all of the makings and let everyone prepare their own meal. It really should be put together at the last minute.

OLIVE SALAD
(TO BE MADE THE DAY BEFORE)

- 3 large cloves garlic, crushed
- 1 cup chopped pimiento-stuffed green olives
- 1 cup pitted and chopped "black-ripe" olives or Calamatas
- ½ cup roasted sweet red peppers cut into chunks
- 1 cup olive oil
- 3 tablespoons chopped fresh parsley
- 2 tablespoons white wine vinegar

Mix all of the above and let stand overnight. Need not be refrigerated for the first night. (You can find the roasted red sweet peppers in jars at any Italian or fancy food shop.)

- 1 large, round, freshly baked Italian bread loaf
- ⅓ pound salami, sliced thin (Genoa or Italian wine-cured)
- ½ pound provolone, sliced thin
- ½ pound mild cheese (such as Havarti), sliced
- ⅓ pound mortadella or prosciutto or coppa or ham, sliced

Cut the bread in half horizontally, as you would for a sandwich. Scoop out some of the center of the loaf and drizzle olive oil from the salad on both halves of the bread. Use plenty! On the bottom half, place the salami, olive salad, provolone, mild cheese, and mortadella. Top with the other half of the loaf. Slice into wedges.

MAY–JUNE

Sunday **27**

Monday **28**

Tuesday **29**

Wednesday **30**

Thursday **31**

FIRST QUARTER

Friday **1**

Saturday **2**

WEDDING AND ENTERTAINING IDEAS

The weeks before your wedding will be a whirlwind of parties! Whether you're hosting a luncheon for the wedding party, planning a get-together for your parents, or entertaining weekend wedding guests, you'll want to follow these tasteful tips. Here's how to serve with style:

- Plan a buffet if you're expecting more than eight guests; you'll have more time to spend with them.

- Select dishes that can be prepared ahead. A variety of main-dish salads is perfect for a bridesmaids' luncheon or shower. Consider baked pasta dishes, casseroles that can be frozen and reheated for a rehearsal dinner.

- Pre-slice meats, cheese before serving them buffet style. It's too difficult for guests to carve while balancing a plate.

- Avoid serving dishes that include runny sauces, or appetizers that have to be "dipped" while guests are standing; someone is bound to spill something.

- Place silverware, condiments, glasses, and beverage pitchers on the dining table so guests don't have to juggle too many items while on the buffet line.

Sunday **3**

Monday **4**

Tuesday **5**

Wednesday **6**

Thursday **7**

Friday **8**

FULL MOON

Saturday **9**

CRAB LOUIS SEATTLE

I cannot think of anything that is more typical of a fine lunch in Seattle than a Crab Louis. This is a grand salad, and a properly prepared one is laden with fresh Dungeness crabmeat. You can use other kinds of crabmeat, of course, but I want to stick to my Dungeness.

CRAB LOUIS DRESSING

1 cup mayonnaise

¼ cup chili sauce (catsup style)

¼ cup whipping cream or half-and-half

1½ tablespoons minced green sweet bell pepper

3 tablespoons peeled and minced yellow onion

1 egg, hard-boiled and grated

1 teaspoon Worcestershire sauce

2 teaspoons chopped fresh parsley

1 tablespoon fresh lemon juice

Salt and freshly ground black pepper to taste

Mix all of the above together and chill.

THE SALAD

Whole iceberg-lettuce leaves to form a basket or bowl for each serving

Shredded iceburg lettuce

Crabmeat, legs included

Sliced hard-boiled eggs

Pitted black olives

Green sweet bell pepper rings

Crab Louis Dressing (above)

Arrange a whole leaf of lettuce on each plate. Use a leaf that is large enough to form a sort of bowl. Put a handful of shredded lettuce in each bowl and then a good serving of crabmeat. Top with sliced eggs, olives, and pepper rings. Pass the dressing and allow your guests to add a bit to their salads.

Sunday **10**

Monday **11**

Tuesday **12**

Wednesday **13**

Thursday **14**

FLAG DAY

Friday **15**

LAST QUARTER

Saturday **16**

RAISIN SCONES

MAKES 12 SCONES

I remember these from the Puyallup County Fair when I was a kid. Just as soon as I had seen the baby pigs I ran to get in line for a scone, a triangular biscuit served hot, filled with butter and raspberry jam. The smell of the hay, the horses, the carnival midway, and the taste of the raspberry jam that stuck to my fingers combined to form a sensuous memory that I doubt I shall ever lose.

This is as close as I can come to that American biscuit product, the scone. I do not think that you need a horse standing around in order to get the full effect.

2 cups flour
$^1/_2$ teaspoon salt
3 teaspoons baking powder
2 tablespoons sugar
$^1/_4$ cup cold butter

$^1/_2$ cup raisins, soaked in hot water for $^1/_2$ hour, drained
$^1/_2$ cup half-and-half or cream
1 egg, beaten

Sift the dry ingredients together. Cut the butter into the dry ingredients, using a pastry blender. Add the drained raisins to the flour mixture. Mix the half-and-half with the beaten egg and stir into the flour mixture. Use a fork and do not overmix. It should take only a few turns to get a dough.

Divide the dough into 3 balls and pat each out into a $^1/_2$-inch-thick circle. Cut each into 4 triangular scones. Bake on an ungreased baking sheet at 450° for about 12 minutes, or until golden brown.

Serve with butter and raspberry jam.

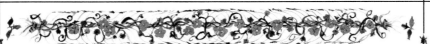

JUNE

Sunday **17**

Monday **18**

Tuesday **19**

Wednesday **20**

Thursday **21**

SUMMER SOLSTICE

Friday **22**

NEW MOON

Saturday **23**

MIDSUMMER'S EVE

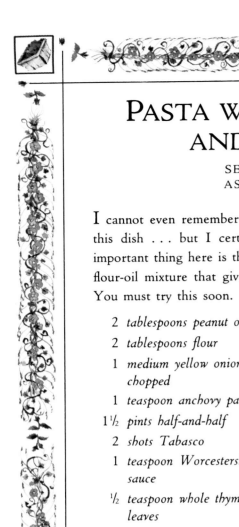

PASTA WITH OYSTERS AND SHRIMP

SERVES 4 TO 5
AS MAIN DISH

I cannot even remember where in New Orleans I first tasted this dish . . . but I certainly remember the dish itself. The important thing here is the cooking of the roux. It is this dark flour-oil mixture that gives the dish both its color and depth. You must try this soon.

2 tablespoons peanut oil

2 tablespoons flour

1 medium yellow onion, chopped

1 teaspoon anchovy paste

1½ pints half-and-half

2 shots Tabasco

1 teaspoon Worcestershire sauce

½ teaspoon whole thyme leaves

1 pint small oysters

1 pound shrimp, raw and peeled (32 to 40 per pound)

Salt and freshly ground black pepper to taste

½ pound cooked pasta

4 green onions, chopped, for garnish

Heat a large frying pan and add the oil. Stir in the flour and cook this mixture until it is the color of light peanut butter, being careful not to burn it. And the onions and sauté until limp. Stir in the anchovy paste and the half-and-half, stirring carefully with a plastic whip to avoid lumps. Turn to a light simmer and add the Tabasco, Worcestershire sauce, and thyme and simmer for 10 minutes. Add the oysters and shrimp and heat for a few minutes. Do not overcook the seafood. Add salt and pepper to taste and serve over the hot pasta. Garnish with chopped green onion.

All you need to complete a menu with this rich dish are a big green salad and a dry white wine.

Sunday 24

Monday 25

Tuesday 26

Wednesday 27

Thursday 28

Friday 29

FIRST QUARTER

Saturday 30

SALMON BARBECUE

SERVES 8

I love to have people from the Midwest come to my house for dinner. Generally they have had little salmon in their time, and very little that was truly fresh. I do not buy a salmon at my fish market unless the creature winks at me! People who have never tasted such a fish are always startled by its wonderful flavor and texture.

1 *whole fresh salmon, about 6 pounds, cleaned*

1 *cup olive oil*

4 *cloves garlic, peeled and crushed*

3 *bunches parsley, washed*

Alder-wood chips or sawdust for barbecuing

Pat the salmon dry with paper towels. Mix the olive oil and garlic together and brush the outside and inside of the fish with the oil. Place the parsley in the stomach cavity of the fish and set it on a large piece of heavy-duty aluminum foil. Roll up the sides of the foil so that you have a very shallow pan around the fish.

Have your barbecue fire ready. I prefer to do this in a Kamado or a covered cooker, such as a Weber. Have the fire at about 375° and place the wood chips on the coals. Soak them first so that they will just smoke rather than ignite. If using sawdust, put it in an old pie pan or aluminum-foil pan and set it on the coals. Place the fish in the cooker and close the lid. Watch the temperature carefully, and in 25 minutes test the fish. The meat should just begin to flake, but still be moist. Remove to a platter and pull the skin off the top side.

You will need no sauce to go with this, as the fish is wonderfully flavored by the smoke and parsley and garlic.

Serve with a great deal of French bread and a large tomato salad. Barbecued zucchini would be delicious.

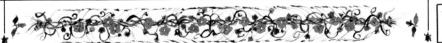

JULY

Sunday **1**

CANADA DAY

Monday **2**

Tuesday **3**

Wednesday **4**

INDEPENDENCE DAY

Thursday **5**

Friday **6**

Saturday **7**

FULL MOON

Corn Chowder with Crawfish

SERVES 8 TO 10

Although this delicious soup is just perfect for a cold winter evening, I made it one day in July and enjoyed it even in the summer heat. It seems that we are getting back to making soup, a food product that our forefathers and foremothers practically lived on.

2 quarts canned chicken broth

1 medium yellow onion, peeled and diced

4 tablespoons butter or olive oil

4 tablespoons flour

2 cups unpeeled diced (¼-inch pieces) potatoes

1 bay leaf

2 cups half-and-half

8 ears fresh corn, scraped from the cob, or 1 bag (20 ounces) frozen corn kernels and 1 can (17 ounces) creamed corn

Salt and freshly ground black pepper to taste

1 pound crawfish tail meat, cooked

4 tablespoons chopped parsley for garnish

3 hard-boiled eggs, peeled and sliced

Place the chicken stock in a 6-quart kettle and put it on to heat.

In a small frying pan sauté the onion in the butter or oil just until clear. Stir in the flour and cook for a moment, thus making a roux. Stir the roux into the hot soup stock, stirring until the soup thickens a bit.

Add the potatoes and bay leaf and cook until the potatoes are tender. Remove the bay leaf.

Add the half-and-half and the corn. Bring to a simmer and season to taste with salt and pepper. I like a bit of extra pepper in this dish. Finally, add the crawfish meat and heat for just a moment. Serve, garnished with the parsley and sliced eggs.

Sunday **8**

Monday **9**

Tuesday **10**

Wednesday **11**

Thursday **12**

Friday **13**

Saturday **14**

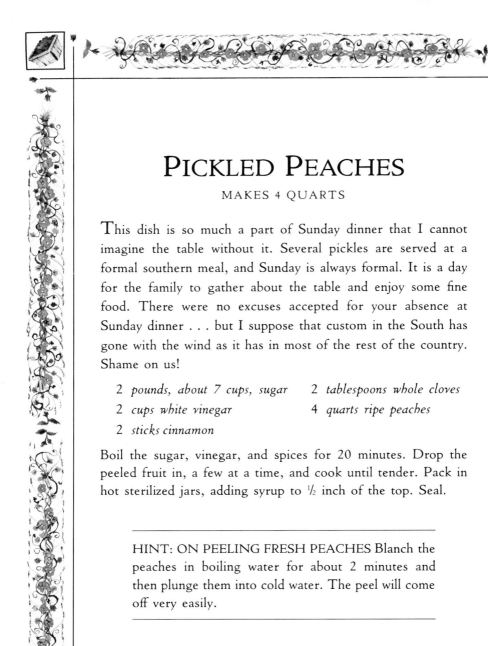

PICKLED PEACHES

MAKES 4 QUARTS

This dish is so much a part of Sunday dinner that I cannot imagine the table without it. Several pickles are served at a formal southern meal, and Sunday is always formal. It is a day for the family to gather about the table and enjoy some fine food. There were no excuses accepted for your absence at Sunday dinner . . . but I suppose that custom in the South has gone with the wind as it has in most of the rest of the country. Shame on us!

2 *pounds, about 7 cups, sugar*	2 *tablespoons whole cloves*
2 *cups white vinegar*	4 *quarts ripe peaches*
2 *sticks cinnamon*	

Boil the sugar, vinegar, and spices for 20 minutes. Drop the peeled fruit in, a few at a time, and cook until tender. Pack in hot sterilized jars, adding syrup to $\frac{1}{2}$ inch of the top. Seal.

HINT: ON PEELING FRESH PEACHES Blanch the peaches in boiling water for about 2 minutes and then plunge them into cold water. The peel will come off very easily.

JULY

Sunday **15**

LAST QUARTER

Monday **16**

Tuesday **17**

Wednesday **18**

Thursday **19**

Friday **20**

Saturday **21**

NEW MOON

STEAMED CLAMS

SERVES 4

Now we are approaching delicate territory. I am a child of the Pacific Northwest, and nobody is allowed to mess with our clams. We like them very close to plain, and that is the way God meant them to be eaten. I know. A very wise old Norwegian told me so.

This is the way that Patty, my wife, likes steamed clams. She is a converted New Yorker, so I now watch her eat them often. Simple to prepare and one of the best seafood dishes I know.

8 pounds steamed clams	½ cup chopped fresh parsley
¼ cup olive oil	1 cup dry white wine
3 cloves garlic, peeled and sliced thin	Black pepper to taste (very little)

Plan on 2 pounds of clams for each person. Wash the clams by stirring them around in a pan in the sink. Keep fresh running water going. Watch for clamshells that are filled with mud. The clam has left home! The mud will ruin your dish. Soak the clams in fresh water for about 1 hour before cooking. They will clean themselves out.

Heat a 12-quart covered soup pot and add the oil and garlic. Cook for a moment and add the remaining ingredients, including the drained clams. Cover and bring to a boil. Stir well once. Cover and simmer for just a few minutes until the clams open. Discard those that do not open. This should take about 8 to 10 minutes.

The stock in the bottom, or nectar, is wonderful. Serve it by the cup with a bit of fresh ground pepper on top.

The clams are eaten from the shell, along with a big green salad, fresh Italian or French bread, and too much beer. This is Seattle/Tacoma heaven.

In my part of the country steamed clams are served with salad and toasted rolls. That's it. If someone orders something in addition to this menu, we know he is from out of town.

VARIATION: Try adding ½ tablespoon whole thyme leaves to this dish. Really very good.

Sunday 22

Monday 23

Tuesday 24

Wednesday 25

Thursday 26

Friday 27

Saturday 28

RASPBERRY ICE

MAKES 2 PINTS

This one came out of an old American cookbook. Our ancestors had to go to a great deal of work to get something that you and I can do in very little time.

- ¼ cup sugar, or to taste
- 1 cup water
- 3 cups raspberry juice or crushed frozen berries, defrosted
- 2 egg whites, beaten

Mix sugar, and juice. Place in freezer. When about frozen, fold in the beaten egg whites. Freeze in a Donvier ice cream machine.

WATERMELON ICE

I did this one morning at my studio, WTTW, Chicago, and the crew could not believe this dish. It is best to make this during the summer when the melons are very ripe.

Remove the rind and all the seeds from an entire watermelon. Purée the pulp in a food processor or food blender. Sweeten to taste and freeze in a Donvier ice cream machine. You may wish to add 2 beaten egg whites. Proceed as above.

GINGER ICE CREAM

MAKES 1 PINT

This is so rich and good that it will start a fight among your children. You scoop it out and divide it. Don't let them even try!

- 1 pint light cream
- ⅛ teaspoon salt
- ½ cup sugar
- 1 tablespoon candied ginger diced very fine

Warm the cream along with the ginger. Do not allow it even to come to a simmer. Stir in the salt and sugar. Allow to cool slowly. Chill. Freeze in a Donvier ice cream machine.

Sunday **29**

FIRST QUARTER

Monday **30**

Tuesday **31**

Wednesday **1**

Thursday **2**

Friday **3**

Saturday **4**

BLACKENED CATFISH

SERVES 6

Okay, so I admit that I too am tired of everyone blackening everything. This method, however, is very easy and the results unusually good. I prefer this to blackened redfish (which is nearing the endangered-species list), blackened chicken, and, Lord save us all, blackened oysters. Why would you do such a thing to a perfectly innocent oyster?

This is the only time that you have ever seen me use garlic and onion powders . . . but this is the only way you can do this dish.

SPICE MIX

- 2 *tablespoons sweet paprika*
- 2½ *tablespoons salt*
- 1 *teaspoon onion powder*
- 1½ *teaspoons garlic powder*
- 1½ *teaspoons cayenne pepper*

- 2 *teaspoons lemon pepper**
- 1 *teaspoon whole thyme leaves*
- 1½ *teaspoons whole basil leaves*

Mix together all the ingredients and store in a lidded jar. You will probably not need all of this mix for a particular recipe. Use it on other meats as well.

- 4 *catfish fillets (total weight about 3 pounds)*
- ½ *stick butter*
- ¼ *cup olive oil*

Heat a black iron frying pan for at least 10 minutes over very high heat.

Cut each of the fillets in half. Melt the butter and mix with the olive oil. Place the spice mix on a plate. Dip the fish into the butter and oil and then dredge on both sides in the spice mix. Fry in a very hot pan just a few minutes on each side. This must be done in a room with a very good kitchen fan or out in the backyard over a very hot charcoal barbecue fire.

Serve this with a great deal of beer, an enormous green salad, and macaroni pie.

*Lemon pepper is a blend that can be found in the spice section of the local supermarket.

Sunday **5**

FRIENDSHIP DAY

Monday **6**

FULL MOON

Tuesday **7**

Wednesday **8**

Thursday **9**

Friday **10**

Saturday **11**

CHICKEN BARBECUED WITH ROSEMARY AND MARSALA

SERVES 2 TO 3

I developed this recipe after having dinner in San Francisco one evening. Harvey Steiman, editor of *Wine Spectator* magazine, was cooking for me in his backyard and he kept adding rosemary branches to the barbecue. The result was a lamb dish that was heaven. If you do not have fresh rosemary growing in your yard, then you can use whole dried rosemary for this dish. However, look into growing rosemary where you are. It will grow to be the size of a hedge in very little time . . . and it needs little care.

MARINADE

4 tablespoons fresh rosemary needles or 2 tablespoons dried rosemary needles

½ cup olive oil

¼ cup dry Marsala wine

4 cloves garlic, peeled and crushed

Juice of 1 lemon

Salt and freshly ground black pepper to taste

Wood chips or sawdust (optional)

2 whole chickens (each about 3 to 3½ pounds)

Mix everything together for the marinade. Cut the chicken in half and marinate for 2 hours.

Cook over a medium fire in your barbecue. If you are using a dome, the fire should be about 375° to 390°. Cook for about 1 hour or until the chicken is done to your taste. Baste the birds with the remaining marinade now and then. If you are using a covered or lidded barbecue, it will not be necessary to turn the chicken. An open barbecue means the chicken must be turned once. If you wish to have a smoky flavor, put some soaked wood chips or sawdust on your charcoal.

I like this with a tomato salad and baked polenta.

Sunday **12**

Monday **13**

LAST QUARTER

Tuesday **14**

Wednesday **15**

Thursday **16**

Friday **17**

Saturday **18**

COLD TOMATO SOUP
GAZPACHO

SERVES 6 TO 8

The argument over this soup is a great deal of fun. It is actually a ground-up salad . . . dressing included. The argument centers not on whether it is a soup or a salad but on whether or not it is Spanish at all. I have located recipes for thirty variations of this stuff, and each maintains that it is the genuine article, and that the dish is a very old tradition in Spain. Other experts maintain that the dish is very new in the culture. One of the first cookbooks to be published in America, *The Virginia Housewife*, lists the dish and says the recipe is from Spain, and that book was published in 1824. Who cares! This is a delicious first course or appetizer . . . or maybe liquid salad. In any case, it will get a Spanish dinner off to the right start because you can serve it in glasses and allow your guests to walk about while they are drinking their salad, or eating their first course . . . having soup.

1 clove garlic, peeled	6 tablespoons wine vinegar, red or white
½ green sweet bell pepper, seeded and cored	½ teaspoon cumin, ground
½ yellow onion, peeled	1 tablespoon Tabasco, or to taste
5 very ripe tomatoes, cored and quartered	Salt and freshly ground black pepper to taste
1 medium cucumber, peeled and sliced	1 cup ice water
	2 cups tomato juice
1 tablespoon tomato paste	2 eggs, hard-boiled, grated for garnish

Blend all the ingredients, except the grated egg, in a food blender or food processor. You will have to do this in several batches. Chill well before serving. Pour in wineglasses or cups and garnish with the grated egg. Leave the wine vinegar and black pepper grinder out so that your guests or family might add a bit to their glasses.

WINE SUGGESTION: Light dry white.

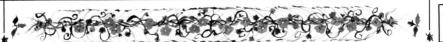

Sunday **19**

Monday **20**

NEW MOON

Tuesday **21**

Wednesday **22**

Thursday **23**

Friday **24**

Saturday **25**

BEEF ON A STICK WITH PEANUT SAUCE

SATÉ

SERVES 5 TO 6

What does a recipe from Indonesia have to do with American cooking? Because peanuts came from the Americas to Indonesia, that's why. And besides, I love this recipe. Great for the barbecue!

1 round steak (2 pounds), trimmed of fat

MARINADE

2 cloves garlic, crushed

1 teaspoon ground coriander

3 tablespoons finely diced yellow onion

1 tablespoon brown sugar

1 teaspoon fresh lemon juice

2 tablespoons light soy sauce

3 tablespoons dry sherry

SAUCE

1 cup dry-roasted unsalted peanuts

½ cup light soy sauce
Dash of Tabasco, or to taste

2 tablespoons light brown sugar

1 tablespoon fresh lemon juice

½ yellow onion, peeled, diced, and pan-fried until brown

Cut the meat into thin strips, being careful to remove the fat. Mix the marinade ingredients and soak the meat strips for at least ½ hour. Put the meat on bamboo skewers in an S pattern.

Prepare the sauce by grinding the peanuts in a food blender or medium-sized food processor. Place in a bowl and add all other ingredients for the sauce.

Broil the sticks of meat over charcoal or under the broiler. Cook just until barely browned, about 4 minutes on each side. You want the meat to be fairly rare and tender.

Spoon the sauce over the meat when you serve.

I like a sliced cucumber salad with a vinaigrette dressing. You need add only plain steamed rice and the menu is complete.

NOTE: This sauce is great on other meat dishes as well. And I love it on fish.

Sunday **26**

Monday **27**

Tuesday **28**

FIRST QUARTER

Wednesday **29**

Thursday **30**

Friday **31**

Saturday **1**

CALIFORNIA CHILI

SERVES 4

This one has to be different. If it came from California, it is unusual and probably has sprouts in it, or at least avocado. Try this. No avocado, but chicken and a very mild chili sauce from a jar. It is really a great dish, although one should not confuse it with the old-line chili cookers' product.

1 pound kidney beans, soaked, cooked, and drained

1 chicken, cut up and browned (I do this in a 400° oven.)

3 tablespoons olive oil

4 cloves garlic, sliced

3 yellow onions, peeled and chopped

1 teaspoon whole cumin seeds

2 jalapeño peppers, seeded and chopped

2 cups chili sauce (catsup section of supermarket)

4 tomatoes, chopped

2 green sweet bell peppers, seeded and chopped

1 tablespoon Worcestershire sauce

1 cup red wine

Salt to taste

Cook the beans and brown the chicken. Heat a large frying pan and add the oil. Sauté the garlic, onions, cumin seeds, and jalapeño peppers until the onions are clear. Add *all* to a heavy pot and bring to a simmer. Cook for 1 hour.

HINT: ON PREPARING COOKED BEANS FOR CHILI WITH BEANS Chili with beans has a much better flavor if you use dried beans and cook them yourself rather than using canned beans. Simply soak the needed amount of red kidney or other beans in ample water overnight. Then simmer until tender. The beans are then drained and added to the chili. Cook the beans in the chili sauce and simmer for 1 to 1½ more hours.

SEPTEMBER

Sunday 2

Monday 3

LABOR DAY

Tuesday 4

FULL MOON

Wednesday 5

Thursday 6

Friday 7

Saturday 8

PASTA AL PESTO

MAKES ABOUT 2 CUPS
SERVES 10 TO 12 AS A PASTA SAUCE

This is one of my favorite pasta dishes. When I don't have the time to grow my own basil, I buy it by the bagful at the Pike Place Farmers Market, a Seattle institution. Buy the basil in the summer, when it is cheap, and prepare and freeze the sauce.

4 cups basil leaves
½ cup olive oil
2 cloves garlic
6 sprigs parsley
Salt and freshly ground black pepper to taste

¼ cup pine nuts, walnuts, or almonds
½ cup freshly grated Parmesan or Romano cheese

Place the basil in a blender (don't bother trying this with dried basil; it won't work). Add the oil, garlic, parsley, salt, pepper, and pine nuts, walnuts, or almonds. Blend until all are chopped very fine. Remove from the blender, and add the Parmesan or Romano cheese.

Toss a little of this great sauce with hot thin spaghetti, and top with a little more cheese. Superb!

HINT: ENJOY OLIVE OIL There is growing evidence that points to olive oil as being quite good for you. It seems to have the ability to help the body clear itself of the harmful part of cholesterol, the part that stays in your arteries as fat. Called a monounsaturated oil, olive oil seems to be more helpful in this cleansing process than even polyunsaturated oils. But oil is oil and we still tend to use too much. Since olive oil has such a bright flavor you may just be better able to cut down by simply using less oil. And olive oil has the advantage of keeping longer than most other oils.

Sunday **9**

Monday **10**

Tuesday **11**

LAST QUARTER

Wednesday **12**

Thursday **13**

Friday **14**

Saturday **15**

CARNE ADOVADO
SERVES 6

When I saw this dish, ready to cook, in the meat shops of Albuquerque I was almost afraid to try it. The dried red peppers make the marinated pork look as if it's hot enough to remove paint from walls! Actually, it's not as hot as you might think. You can vary the spiciness of this basic New Mexico dish simply by choosing hotter or milder dried chile pods. I now make this dish often and I never cease to enjoy it. The flavors are just superb! I believe that the American Indians of the Southwest have one of the richest food backgrounds in America.

BLENDED RED CHILE PODS

7 to 8 *whole dried chile pods, seeded and deveined*

2 *cloves garlic*

1 *teaspoon oregano*

1 *teaspoon salt*

2 *pounds boneless pork butt or shoulder, sliced thin*

Choose the dried chiles for your dish. They range in "heat" from mild to very hot . . . so ask your merchant to point the way.

Prepare the chiles by slitting or cracking them open and removing the seeds and veins. The seeds and veins are what make the chiles hot, so you should clean the peppers according to how hot you wish them to be. Place the chile skins in a bowl and add enough hot tap water to cover. Allow them to sit for 1 hour and then drain, reserving the liquid. Place the pepper skins in a blender and add enough of the water to bring the total amount in your machine to 1 pint. Add the garlic, oregano, and salt. Blend until thick and smooth.

Place the sliced pork in a stainless steel bowl and pour in the chili sauce. Mix the meat and marinade and cover. Refrigerate overnight.

When ready to cook, heat oven to 350°. Place meat and marinade in a covered casserole and bake at 350° for 1 hour. Wonderful, and not as hot as it looks.

I like this with corn bread and sweet potatoes and onions. This should sound a little heavy to you, so add a green salad. See what I care!

Sunday **16**

MEXICAN INDEPENDENCE DAY

Monday **17**

Tuesday **18**

NEW MOON

Wednesday **19**

Thursday **20**

FIRST DAY OF ROSH HASHANAH

Friday **21**

Saturday **22**

GEFILTE FISH

MAKES 20

Mrs. Morris Kleiner, of Tacoma, a most gracious woman whom I have known since my college days, gave me a lesson in making gefilte fish. Mine is almost as good as hers!

3 pounds fish*	1 teaspoon sugar
1 large or 2 small yellow onions, peeled	Salt and freshly ground black pepper to taste
3 eggs	Fish Stock for Gefilte Fish (below)
¼ to ¾ cup matzo meal	
1 cup cold water	

Put the fish and onion through a meat grinder, or have the fishmonger grind the fish for you. Place the mixture in a bowl, add the other ingredients, and mix thoroughly. Do not use all the matzo meal at once because you may not need much in order to make a firm and workable fish paste. Season generously with salt and pepper. Form into balls, and cook in the fish stock. Let come to a boil; then cook slowly for 1 hour with a lid on the kettle.

Serve the fish cold in some of the broth. Traditionally horse-radish is served on the side.

*Use a mixture of different types such as red salmon, white salmon, cod, or any others you prefer.

FISH STOCK FOR GEFILTE FISH

Fish skin, bones, and heads	4 celery stalks, chopped
2 carrots, cut up	Salt to taste
2 small yellow onions, peeled and chopped	

Cover all ingredients with water, and simmer until the vegetables are soft. Strain, and use the liquid for cooking the gefilte fish balls.

Sunday **23**

AUTUMNAL EQUINOX

Monday **24**

Tuesday **25**

Wednesday **26**

FIRST QUARTER

Thursday **27**

Friday **28**

Saturday **29**

YOM KIPPUR

APPLE COBBLER

SERVES 6 TO 8

We know that the apple seeds brought from England were intended for this very dish. Apple cobbler goes back to the time of the Pilgrims, and since it is so easy to make you should offer this bit of edible history to your family very soon.

3 tablespoons butter for sautéing the apples

2 pounds cooking apples, cored, peeled, and sliced

1/2 cup raisins

1 1/4 cups sugar

1/4 teaspoon ground cinnamon

1/8 teaspoon ground nutmeg

1/4 pound butter, melted (Use microwave.)

1 cup flour

2 teaspoons baking powder

1 teaspoon salt

1/4 cup milk

Vanilla ice cream or whipped cream for topping

Heat a frying pan and add the 3 tablespoons butter. Put the apples and raisins in the pan and sauté for a few minutes over medium heat until they are tender. Add 1/4 cup of the sugar, and the spices. Stir and set aside.

Pour the melted butter into a 7 × 11 × 2-inch baking dish. Mix the remaining cup of sugar with the flour, baking powder, and salt. Mix well and then stir in the milk. Spread this batter on top of the butter.

Pour the apple mixture over the batter and bake in a 350° oven for about 50 minutes, or until the crust is golden brown.

Serve this warm, topped with vanilla ice cream or whipped cream.

Sunday **30**

Monday **1**

Tuesday **2**

Wednesday **3**

Thursday **4**

FULL MOON

Friday **5**

Saturday **6**

SAUTÉED SQUASH

SERVES 4 TO 6

You can also add parsley and carrots to this dish; cook the carrots separately. Once I added a whipped egg at the very last minute.

All possibilities will go well for you as long as you remember the cardinal rule concerning the cooking of light summer squashes: *Don't.* Don't cook to death. Rather simply get it hot and serve it.

3 *small zucchini*
1 *medium yellow summer squash*
2 *tablespoons peanut oil*
2 *cloves garlic, sliced thin*
1 *yellow onion, peeled and sliced thin*
2 *ounces dried mushrooms, soaked in warm water, drained, and chopped, or ½ pound mushrooms, sliced*

Salt and freshly ground black pepper to taste
2 *tablespoons freshly grated Parmesan or Romano cheese*
3 *tablespoons white wine*
3 *tablespoons whipping cream*

Cut the squashes into matchsticks, or use a very coarse grater. Heat the oil in a large frying pan or wok, and sauté the garlic and onion until barely tender.

Add the squashes, mushrooms, salt, and pepper, and sauté for a few minutes until the vegetables are hot. Add the cream and white wine. Cook for a moment, and place in a serving bowl. Top with cheese.

Sunday **7**

Monday **8**

COLUMBUS DAY
THANKSGIVING DAY *(Canada)*

Tuesday **9**

Wednesday **10**

LAST QUARTER

Thursday **11**

Friday **12**

Saturday **13**

PUMPKIN SOUFFLÉ

SERVES 6

This lovely dish can be served year-round if you have prepared some puréed pumpkin and stored it in your freezer. Otherwise, use canned. People will be impressed with this dish on a cold January evening, as it is rich and warming. *Warming* is a Colonial term for serious food!

2 tablespoons butter
¼ cup finely chopped yellow onion
2 teaspoons flour
½ cup whipping cream
1½ cups puréed pumpkin (canned will work)
½ teaspoon salt
¼ teaspoon freshly ground black pepper

¼ teaspoon freshly grated nutmeg
Cayenne pepper to taste
4 egg yolks, lightly beaten
6 egg whites at room temperature
¼ teaspoon cream of tartar

In a frying pan, sauté the onion in the butter until transparent. Add the flour and cook until the flour and butter begin to turn a very light golden brown. Using a whisk, add the cream and cook until a thick sauce is obtained. Pour this sauce into a medium-sized mixing bowl and add the remaining ingredients, except the eggs and cream of tartar. Mix well. Then stir in the egg yolks, one at a time. A mixer is great for this.

Whip the egg whites along with the cream of tartar and gently fold into the pumpkin mixture. Do not overmix. Place in a buttered 1½-quart soufflé dish and bake in a preheated oven at 350° for about 30 minutes, or until the soufflé begins to expand and brown ever so slightly on top. Serve right away.

Serve this as a vegetable course at a light dinner. It is rich enough to stand up against anything!

Sunday **14**

Monday **15**

Tuesday **16**

Wednesday **17**

Thursday **18**

NEW MOON

Friday **19**

Saturday **20**

WHAT TO SERVE AT A WINE TASTING

You *cannot* have it all—not all at the same time, anyway. You cannot do justice to the evaluation of wine and enjoy wonderful, flavorful food simultaneously. The reason, of course, is that food changes the flavor of the wine, which after all it's supposed to. So, what to serve at wine tasting to sustain the body without wrecking the palate?

The traditional prescription of bread and cheese is a good one, within limits. First, the bread should be plain—a French- or Italian-style loaf is best. It should not be too salty, as salt tends to dull the palate. Chewing on a bit of bread between glasses of wine performs a valuable service—it cleans the palate of wine flavors and prepares you to taste the next wine without being prejudiced by the previous one. (Water does the same thing, but I find that, particularly with strongly flavored wines, bread is best.)

Cheese makes a wonderful accompaniment to wine—but beware. Cheese is so good with wine that it tends to deceive one about the taste of the wine itself. And a strong-flavored and aromatic cheese—sharp, Cheddar, blue cheese, even Swiss cheese—may cause you to miss a lot of subtle flavors in wine altogether, rather like visiting the Louvre with your sunglasses on. If you're going to serve cheese, then stick to the very mild, creamy ones—like Havarti, or mozzarella, or fresh goat cheese. These will provide enough stimulus to your taste buds to keep them going, without overwhelming them.

Now, of course, there are some exceptions, notably with dessert wines. A number of sweet, full-flavored dessert wines cry out for flavorful cheese to serve with them, even at a tasting. Sauternes and blue cheese is not only a combination created in heaven, but the cheese seems to draw out the flavors of the wine, which by themselves might be overwhelming. Something similar happens with vintage port, which softens and opens up with a nice, smelly cheese like Stilton or very old cheddar. Here again, the wine itself can so easily stun the palate that it is helpful to have something to counterbalance it. Don't, incidentally, try to mix a tasting of dessert wines with dinner wines—your mouth will never forgive you.

Sunday **21**

Monday **22**

Tuesday **23**

Wednesday **24**

U.N. DAY

Thursday **25**

Friday **26**

FIRST QUARTER

Saturday **27**

GERMAN DUMPLINGS
SPAETZLE

SERVES 4

These are little fat noodles that can be made in a hurry. They are a basic in the German diet and go very well with many gravies and sauces.

2 eggs, beaten	½ teaspoon baking powder
½ cup milk	Pinch of grated nutmeg
2 tablespoons water	
1½ cups flour	2 quarts boiling salted water
½ teaspoon salt	5 tablespoons butter
	½ cup toasted bread crumbs

Beat the eggs and add the milk and water. Stir in the flour, salt, baking powder, and nutmeg, mixing well. Bring the water to a boil and add 2 teaspoons salt. The spaetzle should be light and delicious, so check the batter by dropping ½ teaspoon into the boiling water. Cook for 6 to 8 minutes and check the noodle. If it is not light, add a couple more tablespoons of water to the batter. Force the dough through a spaetzle maker or use a plastic bag for forming the noodles. Put all the dough into a heavy 1-quart self-sealing plastic food bag and cut one corner off. Make the cut fairly small so that you can extrude noodles about the size of a pencil. Squeeze on the bag and cut the noodles off into 1-inch pieces. Do this quickly into the boiling water. Boil 6 to 8 minutes. Remove and drain. Heat a large frying pan and melt the butter. Lightly brown the spaetzle in the butter. Top with the bread crumbs and serve.

I like this dish with basic brown sauce or brown gravy.

Sunday **28**

Monday **29**

Tuesday **30**

Wednesday **31**

HALLOWEEN

Thursday **1**

Friday **2**

FULL MOON

Saturday **3**

CRANBERRY BREAD

MAKES 1 LOAF

This is one of the most delicious breakfast breads I know, and I like it best toasted. The simplicity of the Shaker community gathering for prayers and breakfast before a day at hard work must have been a wonderful thing. What ever happened to our morning family time together? It is gone and we may have to reschedule our lives in order to retrieve that precious time.

2 cups flour

½ teaspoon salt

½ teaspoon baking soda

1 cup sugar

1½ teaspoons baking powder
    Juice and grated rind of 1 orange

1 egg, beaten

2 tablespoons melted shortening or salad oil

1 cup fresh or frozen cranberries, coarsely ground

½ cup walnut meats, coarsely chopped

Mix dry ingredients together very well in a large mixing bowl. Put the juice and grated rind in a measuring cup and add enough boiling water to make ¾ cups liquid. Add to the dry mixture. Add the egg and shortening or oil and mix just enough to moisten the flour mixture. Add cranberries and nut meats. Bake in a greased loaf pan 60 to 70 minutes at 325°. Store 24 hours before cutting.

Sunday **4**

Monday **5**

Tuesday **6**

ELECTION DAY

Wednesday **7**

Thursday **8**

Friday **9**

LAST QUARTER

Saturday **10**

INDIAN PUDDING

SERVES 8 TO 10

Cornmeal was originally called Indian meal, since it was a gift from the Indians. The early recipes for this dish do not call for spices, of course, but this old New England version is very delicious. I like the addition of the cinnamon and nutmeg.

1 cup yellow cornmeal
½ cup black molasses
¼ cup sugar
¼ cup butter
¼ teaspoon salt
¼ teaspoon baking soda
2 eggs, beaten

½ teaspoon ground cinnamon
¼ teaspoon freshly grated nutmeg
6 cups hot milk
Vanilla ice cream for topping

Mix the cornmeal with the molasses, sugar, butter, salt, baking soda, eggs, and spices. Add 3 cups of the hot milk, stirring carefully. Place in a 2-quart bean pot or other covered pot and bake in a 400° oven until all comes to a boil. Then stir in the remaining hot milk and bake, covered, at 275° for 4 to 6 hours, or until all is absorbed. Stir every half hour.

Serve hot in little bowls with a bit of vanilla ice cream on top.

NOVEMBER

Sunday **11**

VETERANS DAY
REMEMBRANCE DAY *(Canada)*

Monday **12**

Tuesday **13**

Wednesday **14**

Thursday **15**

Friday **16**

Saturday **17**

NEW MOON

ROAST TURKEY WITH SHERRY BUTTER

SERVES 8 TO 10

The turkeys that the Pilgrims ate must have been terribly stringy and tough old birds. In our time we have developed a lovely bird, and there is simply no excuse for dry turkey meat. You can use either a frozen or a fresh turkey in this recipe, and the injection of butter and sherry will promise you a moist and lovely feast.

1 9- to 12-pound turkey	1 *stick butter or ¹/₂ cup olive*
Salt and freshly ground	*or vegetable oil*
black pepper to taste	¹/₂ *cup dry cocktail sherry*

Clean the bird and remove the giblets. Save the giblets and neck for soup stock. Remove the wing tips, or first section of the wing, and add to the soup stock. Salt and pepper the bird inside and out, and stuff, if you wish.

After stuffing, secure the opening with string or thread, or simply close the opening by folding the skin over it and securing the legs. Instructions are generally included with the bird. Tie the wings to the body, and the legs together. Melt the butter and allow to cool for a few minutes (or use oil). Stir in the dry sherry. Using an injecting needle or plastic flavor injector (available in most gourmet shops), inject the butter and sherry mixture into each of the legs, the thighs, and finally the breast. Just put a bit in 2 or 3 places in each of the mentioned parts. Rub the bird with a bit more butter or oil and roast in your usual manner.

I bake the bird at 325°, uncovered, about 15 minutes a pound. If you are stuffing the bird, add 1 hour for the dressing. A 9- to 12-pound stuffed bird will take between 3¹/₂ and 4 hours. A meat thermometer placed in the thigh should register 180°. Baste the bird with its own juices 2 or 3 times during the roasting.

NOVEMBER

Sunday **18**

Monday **19**

Tuesday **20**

Wednesday **21**

Thursday **22**

THANKSGIVING DAY

Friday **23**

Saturday **24**

SWEET POTATO PIE

SERVES 8

This pie is truly American. Its roots are in soul cooking, and I expect that everyone in your household will love it. The addition of a heavy shot of bourbon, another very American ingredient, gives this pie a very special flavor. Don't worry about the bourbon if you are feeding this to children. The alcohol cooks out completely, but the flavor of the bourbon remains.

2 cups cooked, peeled, and mashed sweet potatoes

4 tablespoons butter or margarine

3 eggs, beaten

1 cup sugar

1 teaspoon vanilla

1 teaspoon freshly grated nutmeg

1 tablespoon fresh lemon juice

½ cup bourbon whiskey

1 unbaked pie shell

Boil the sweet potatoes until very tender, then peel and mash them well. Mix all ingredients together and place in an unbaked pie shell. Place in a 400° oven and immediately turn the oven to 325°. Bake for about 45 minutes or until the center of the pie is set. Test this by inserting a table knife into the center of the pie. If it comes out clean the pie is finished.

Serve with whipped cream or ice cream on top.

NOTE: Any leftover filling can be baked in a baking dish and served as a pudding.

Sunday 25

FIRST QUARTER

Monday 26

Tuesday 27

Wednesday 28

Thursday 29

Friday 30

Saturday 1

SALMON AND CREAM CHEESE BALL

SERVES 16 TO 20 ON HORS D'OEUVRES BUFFET

SERVES 8 AS FIRST COURSE AT DINNER PARTY

SERVES 1 IF JEFF SMITH IS PRESENT

This one is from my mother, Emily Smith. She is the one who taught me the meaning of *frugal* as she is a tough Norwegian . . . and a fine cook. She is one of those people who can go into an empty kitchen and prepare a lovely meal for 8. This is great for an hors d'oeuvres buffet or as a first course at a nice dinner party.

1½ *pounds fresh salmon roast* or *1 pound canned salmon*

½ *teaspoon liquid smoke*

1 *tablespoon horseradish*

1 *tablespoon lemon juice*

½ *pound cream cheese, mashed*

2 *tablespoons mayonnaise*

1 *tablespoon dried parsley flakes*

Steam the fersh salmon for about 45 minutes in a metal steamer. Cool the fish. Skin the salmon, remove the bones, and place the meat in a bowl. Add the remaining ingredients, and mix well.

Sunday 2

FIRST SUNDAY OF ADVENT
FULL MOON

Monday 3

Tuesday 4

Wednesday 5

Thursday 6

Friday 7

Saturday 8

LAST QUARTER

PEARS POACHED IN PORT

SERVES 6

This dish is easy and dramatic. It draws upon the wonderful flavor and depth of the port and the fruitiness and sweetness of the pear. Have everything done ahead of time and you can turn this on to cook as you are clearing the table for dessert.

1 *cup sugar*
1 *pint water*
1 *cinnamon stick*
4 *cloves*
1 *piece fresh orange peel, 1 inch long*
6 *pears, ripe but firm*
1 *cup port, tawny or ruby*

In a saucepan just large enough to take the pears comfortably, mix the sugar, water, cinnamon stick, cloves, and orange peel. Bring to a simmer and then cool.

Peel the pears, leaving the stem intact, if you were lucky enough to find pears that still had their stems. Cut a bit off the bottom of the pear so that it will stand upright in the port and in the serving dish. Leave them set in a stainless or glass bowl covered with mild salt water until ready to cook.

When ready to cook, drain the pears and place them in the sugar syrup pan, upright. Add the port and bring the whole to a gentle boil. Turn to a simmer and cover. Cook until the pears are tender but still a bit firm, about 15 minutes.

Serve each pear upright in a small glass bowl or dish. You might put a puddle of the port broth in the bottom of the dish.

Sunday **9**

Monday **10**

Tuesday **11**

Wednesday **12**

FIRST DAY OF HANUKKAH

Thursday **13**

Friday **14**

Saturday **15**

BRUNCH EGGNOG

SERVES 6 TO 8

This is a gift to us from the Wine Institute in San Francisco. Brian St. Pierre and the bunch there have been most kind to me . . . and I do love California wines. So here is a knockout for a brunch with friends. No, Patty and I do *not* have this each morning for breakfast, although we do share a breakfast cocktail of half champagne and half orange juice now and then.

1 *bottle (750 ml) California cream sherry*

4 *eggs*

1 *can (6 ounce) frozen orange juice concentrate*

2 *cups crushed ice*

Whip the ingredients smooth in a blender, using half amounts each time. Serve in chilled wineglasses.

HINT: CURE FOR THE COMMON COLD? One of our viewers maintains this works. I tried it and liked it, although I didn't have a cold to start with and this drink didn't give me one. So who knows? Mix equal parts orange juice and tawny port together. It looks terrible but it is supposed to help that old cold.

Sunday **16**

NEW MOON

Monday **17**

Tuesday **18**

Wednesday **19**

Thursday **20**

Friday **21**

WINTER SOLSTICE

Saturday **22**

CONFIT OF GOOSE
CONFIT D'OIE

SERVES 6 OR MORE

This is the most common form of confit to be found in France. Geese are hard to find in this country, however, so warn your butcher ahead of time and he will locate a frozen bird for you.

1 *whole goose, defrosted if frozen*

2 *bay leaves*

1 *teaspoon dried whole thyme leaves*

1 *teaspoon dried whole rosemary leaves*

3 *tablespoons salt*

Remove the giblets from the bird and reserve for another use. You might also wish to remove the tips of the wings and reserve them for soup. Remove all fat that you can see from the rear end and the neck area of the goose. Save the fat in the refrigerator. You might also save the skin of the neck, which is very fatty.

Cut the goose up into 6 to 8 equal pieces. Mix the herbs with the salt, crushing the herbs as you mix. Dry the goose pieces with paper towels and rub each with the salt/herb mixture. Place the pieces in a glass or stainless steel bowl and cover with a plate. Place a weight on the top, such as a brick, and refrigerate for 2 days.

To cook: Place a large Dutch oven or metal casserole on the stove and add to it all of the reserved fat. Add 1 cup water. Heat slowly so that the fat is rendered without burning. This will take about $\frac{1}{2}$ hour over moderate heat (medium low). Cover the pan during this process.

Rinse the salt and herbs from the meat and dry each piece. Place the meat in the pot and turn each so that it is coated with fat. Cover and cook over moderate heat for $2\frac{1}{2}$ hours, or until the goose is very tender when pierced with a pot fork. Watch the pot closely during this entire time so that the meat does not overly brown or go dry. You may need to lower the heat or turn the meat once.

The meat can be served at this point, but it is much better if you place the meat in a glass or stainless bowl and pour the fat over the meat. Allow it to sit in the refrigerator in its own fat for anywhere from 1 to 3 days. When ready to serve, remove a piece, sauté it in a pan, browning lightly, and serve.

The meat can also be used in salads, soups, and stews. It is particularly good with bean dishes.

Sunday 23

Monday 24

CHRISTMAS EVE
FIRST QUARTER

Tuesday 25

CHRISTMAS

Wednesday 26

BOXING DAY (*Canada*)

Thursday 27

Friday 28

Saturday 29

OYSTERS IN CHAMPAGNE SAUCE

SERVES 4 TO 5

My wife and I were fascinated by a restaurant in Tours, France. Called The Pepper Mill, it is run by an Englishwoman and her French husband, the chef. She served a dish to us that was similar to the one here. It was delicious, but she told us how difficult it was for her to get the French to eat a *cooked* oyster. She is having success with this dish:

2 *tablespoons butter or olive oil*	1 *pound fresh spinach, carefully washed*
2 *garlic cloves, peeled and sliced*	1 *tablespoon* each *butter and flour cooked together for a roux*
1 *cup dry champagne*	
½ *cup whipping cream*	*Salt to taste*
1 *pound small oysters*	

In an enamel or stainless pan, melt the butter and sauté the sliced garlic for a moment. Add the liquid from the oysters along with the champagne and cream. Simmer to reduce by about one third liquid volume. Add the oysters to the sauce. Place the spinach on top and cover. Cook for just a moment. You do not want to overcook the oysters.

Remove the lid and place the spinach on a heated plate. With a slotted spoon remove the oysters and place them on the spinach bed. Thicken the sauce with the roux and pour the sauce over the oysters.

Serve with risotto with mushrooms, a green salad with pesto vinaigrette dressing, and French rolls.

WINE SUGGESTION: French Chablis or Chardonnay.

Sunday 30

Monday 31

FULL MOON

1989

JANUARY

S	M	T	W	T	F	S
1	2	3	4	5	6	7
8	9	10	11	12	13	14
15	16	17	18	19	20	21
22	23	24	25	26	27	28
29	30	31				

MARCH

S	M	T	W	T	F	S
			1	2	3	4
5	6	7	8	9	10	11
12	13	14	15	16	17	18
19	20	21	22	23	24	25
26	27	28	29	30	31	

MAY

S	M	T	W	T	F	S
	1	2	3	4	5	6
7	8	9	10	11	12	13
14	15	16	17	18	19	20
21	22	23	24	25	26	27
28	29	30	31			

JULY

S	M	T	W	T	F	S
						1
2	3	4	5	6	7	8
9	10	11	12	13	14	15
16	17	18	19	20	21	22
23	24	25	26	27	28	29
30	31					

SEPTEMBER

S	M	T	W	T	F	S
					1	2
3	4	5	6	7	8	9
10	11	12	13	14	15	16
17	18	19	20	21	22	23
24	25	26	27	28	29	30

NOVEMBER

S	M	T	W	T	F	S
			1	2	3	4
5	6	7	8	9	10	11
12	13	14	15	16	17	18
19	20	21	22	23	24	25
26	27	28	29	30		

IMPORTANT DATES

JANUARY
1 New Year's Day
16 Martin Luther King's Birthday (Observed)

FEBRUARY
8 Ash Wednesday
12 Lincoln's Birthday
14 Valentine's Day
20 Washington's Birthday (Observed)

MARCH
5 Mothering Sunday (U.K.)
17 St. Patrick's Day
19 Palm Sunday
24 Good Friday
26 Easter
27 Easter Monday (Canada)

APRIL
2 Daylight Saving Time Begins
20 First Day of Passover

MAY
1 May Day Holiday (U.K.)
14 Mother's Day
20 Armed Forces Day
22 Victoria Day (Canada)
29 Memorial Day
29 Spring Holiday (U.K. not Scotland)

JUNE
5 Holiday (Republic of Ireland)
14 Flag Day
18 Father's Day

JULY
1 Canada Day
4 Independence Day
12 Holiday (N. Ireland)

AUGUST
7 Holiday (Republic of Ireland)
28 Late Summer Holiday (U.K. not Scotland)

SEPTEMBER
4 Labor Day
30 First Day of Rosh Hashanah

OCTOBER
9 Yom Kippur
9 Columbus Day
9 Thanksgiving Day (Canada)
29 Daylight Saving Time Ends
31 Halloween

NOVEMBER
5 Election Day
11 Veterans Day
11 Remembrance Day (Canada)
23 Thanksgiving Day

DECEMBER
23 First Day of Hanukkah
25 Christmas
26 Boxing Day

FEBRUARY

S	M	T	W	T	F	S
			1	2	3	4
5	6	7	8	9	10	11
12	13	14	15	16	17	18
19	20	21	22	23	24	25
26	27	28				

APRIL

S	M	T	W	T	F	S
						1
2	3	4	5	6	7	8
9	10	11	12	13	14	15
16	17	18	19	20	21	22
23	24	25	26	27	28	29
30						

JUNE

S	M	T	W	T	F	S
				1	2	3
4	5	6	7	8	9	10
11	12	13	14	15	16	17
18	19	20	21	22	23	24
25	26	27	28	29	30	

AUGUST

S	M	T	W	T	F	S
		1	2	3	4	5
6	7	8	9	10	11	12
13	14	15	16	17	18	19
20	21	22	23	24	25	26
27	28	29	30	31		

OCTOBER

S	M	T	W	T	F	S
1	2	3	4	5	6	7
8	9	10	11	12	13	14
15	16	17	18	19	20	21
22	23	24	25	26	27	28
29	30	31				

DECEMBER

S	M	T	W	T	F	S
					1	2
3	4	5	6	7	8	9
10	11	12	13	14	15	16
17	18	19	20	21	22	23
24	25	26	27	28	29	30
31						

1991

JANUARY

S	M	T	W	T	F	S
		1	2	3	4	5
6	7	8	9	10	11	12
13	14	15	16	17	18	19
20	21	22	23	24	25	26
27	28	29	30	31		

MARCH

S	M	T	W	T	F	S
					1	2
3	4	5	6	7	8	9
10	11	12	13	14	15	16
17	18	19	20	21	22	23
24	25	26	27	28	29	30
31						

MAY

S	M	T	W	T	F	S
			1	2	3	4
5	6	7	8	9	10	11
12	13	14	15	16	17	18
19	20	21	22	23	24	25
26	27	28	29	30	31	

JULY

S	M	T	W	T	F	S
	1	2	3	4	5	6
7	8	9	10	11	12	13
14	15	16	17	18	19	20
21	22	23	24	25	26	27
28	29	30	31			

SEPTEMBER

S	M	T	W	T	F	S
1	2	3	4	5	6	7
8	9	10	11	12	13	14
15	16	17	18	19	20	21
22	23	24	25	26	27	28
29	30					

NOVEMBER

S	M	T	W	T	F	S
					1	2
3	4	5	6	7	8	9
10	11	12	13	14	15	16
17	18	19	20	21	22	23
24	25	26	27	28	29	30

IMPORTANT DATES

JANUARY
1 New Year's Day
21 Martin Luther King's
   Birthday (Observed)

FEBRUARY
12 Lincoln's Birthday
13 Ash Wednesday
14 Valentine's Day
18 Washington's Birthday
   (Observed)

MARCH
10 Mothering Sunday (U.K.)
17 St. Patrick's Day
24 Palm Sunday
29 Good Friday
30 First Day of Passover
31 Easter

APRIL
1 Easter Monday (Canada)
7 Daylight Saving Time Begins

MAY
6 May Day Holiday (U.K.)
12 Mother's Day
18 Armed Forces Day
20 Victoria Day (Canada)
27 Memorial Day
27 Spring Holiday
   (U.K. not Scotland)

JUNE
3 Holiday (Republic of Ireland)
14 Flag Day
16 Father's Day

JULY
1 Canada Day
4 Independence Day
12 Holiday (N. Ireland)

AUGUST
5 Holiday (Republic of Ireland)
26 Late Summer Holiday
   (U.K. not Scotland)

SEPTEMBER
2 Labor Day
9 First Day of Rosh Hashanah
18 Yom Kippur

OCTOBER
14 Columbus Day
14 Thanksgiving Day (Canada)
27 Daylight Saving Time Ends
31 Halloween

NOVEMBER
5 Election Day
11 Veterans Day
11 Remembrance Day (Canada)
28 Thanksgiving Day

DECEMBER
2 First Day of Hanukkah
25 Christmas
26 Boxing Day

FEBRUARY

S	M	T	W	T	F	S
					1	2
3	4	5	6	7	8	9
10	11	12	13	14	15	16
17	18	19	20	21	22	23
24	25	26	27	28		

APRIL

S	M	T	W	T	F	S
	1	2	3	4	5	6
7	8	9	10	11	12	13
14	15	16	17	18	19	20
21	22	23	24	25	26	27
28	29	30				

JUNE

S	M	T	W	T	F	S
						1
2	3	4	5	6	7	8
9	10	11	12	13	14	15
16	17	18	19	20	21	22
23	24	25	26	27	28	29
30						

AUGUST

S	M	T	W	T	F	S
				1	2	3
4	5	6	7	8	9	10
11	12	13	14	15	16	17
18	19	20	21	22	23	24
25	26	27	28	29	30	31

OCTOBER

S	M	T	W	T	F	S
		1	2	3	4	5
6	7	8	9	10	11	12
13	14	15	16	17	18	19
20	21	22	23	24	25	26
27	28	29	30	31		

DECEMBER

S	M	T	W	T	F	S
1	2	3	4	5	6	7
8	9	10	11	12	13	14
15	16	17	18	19	20	21
22	23	24	25	26	27	28
29	30	31				

Also available from William Morrow

THE FRUGAL GOURMET

JEFF SMITH

Jeff Smith's first cookbook companion to his 13-part national television series, spent more than a year on *The New York Times* best-seller list and has sold more than one million copies. With over 400 recipes from a rich assortment of international cuisines, including many low-salt and low-fat dishes, *The Frugal Gourmet* shows what *frugal* really means: getting the most out of your time, your money, and your kitchen.

Also available from William Morrow

THE
FRUGAL GOURMET
COOKS WITH WINE
JEFF SMITH

Jeff Smith's second cookbook companion to his 26-part national television series, features more than 300 exciting recipes from appetizers to desserts, many of which call for wine as an essential ingredient. With the Frugal Gourmet at your side, you'll learn how wine allows you to cook more creatively while cutting down on your desire for salt—*without alcohol*, which evaporates during cooking. Let Jeff Smith show you why wine deserves a place on every pantry shelf and hear his solid advice on wine tasting, how to select wine, what to serve it with, even how to survive the sommelier in a restaurant! *The Frugal Gourmet Cooks with Wine* spent a year on *The New York Times* best-seller list and has sold nearly a million copies.

Also available from William Morrow

THE
FRUGAL GOURMET
COOKS AMERICAN

JEFF SMITH

Jeff Smith is blatant and open about his new cookbook. "It's an attempt at cooking patriotism!" Featuring more than 350 recipes, the book celebrates corn, turkey, tomatoes, squashes, peanuts, maple syrup, chocolate, and other foods that are "strictly American." Companion to the all-new 39-part national television series, Jeff's third book, *The Frugal Gourmet Cooks American,* is also fun and interesting reading about America's culinary history.

Also available from William Morrow

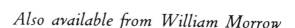

THE FRUGAL GOURMET COOKS THREE ANCIENT CUISINES: CHINA, GREECE, AND ROME

JEFF SMITH

Jeff Smith believes in giving culinary credit where it is due. In his fourth cookbook, he features the cuisines of China, Greece, and Rome, the three cultures that had the greatest influence on western cuisine as we know it. Join the Frugal Gourmet as he visits these exotic lands and prepares the authentic dishes that are their legacy to the West: eggplant, lamb, exotic breads, dim sum, mushrooms, dumplings, desserts, and more.

Companion to the all-new 39-part PBS television series.

NOTES